A New True Book

THE INCA

By Patricia McKissack

CHILDRENS PRESS ®

CHICAGO

Reed boats in Lake Titicaca in Bolivia

PHOTO CREDITS

Historical Pictures Service—21 (left), 41 (2 photos), 43

Roloc Color Slides—2, 11 (right), 14 (right), 31, 36 (right), 37 (right)

Root Resources—37 (left)

Nawrocki Stock Photo—
© D. Variakojis—4, 25

Hillstrom Stock Photo:
© Steve Carr Photo—6, 24 (right), 30 (2 photos), 45
© Connie McCollum—11 (left), 14 (left), 19 (left), 26 (top-left)
© Blehert/Koehn Photography—12 (right), 24 (left), 26 (top-right), 44 (left)
© Charles Fernandez—23 (left)

The Granger Collection—12 (left), 34 (2 photos), 38, 40

Chip & Rosa Maria Peterson—17 (2 photos), 21 (right), 23 (right), 35, 44 (right)

Tom Stack & Associates—19 (right), 26 (bottom), 28 (2 photos), 32
© Allin—36 (left)

Virginia Grimes—Cover

Len Meents—8

COVER—Women tending llamas

Library of Congress Cataloging in Publication Data

McKissack, Pat, 1944-
   The Inca.

   Includes index.
   Summary: Traces the rise of the Incan civilization with emphasis on their culture, social structure, government, economy, and the fatal encounter with the Spanish conquistadors which brought about the end of their society.
   1. Incas—Juvenile literature. [1. Incas. [2. Indians of South America] I. Title.
F3429.M43   1985   985'.01   85-6712
ISBN 0-516-01268-1   AACR2

TABLE OF CONTENTS

The Inca built Machu Picchu on top of a mountain about fifty miles from Cuzco, Peru. Hiram Bingham discovered this ancient city in 1911.

CHILDREN OF THE SUN

People lived in the Andes Mountains of Peru as early as 5000 B.C. They lived in small tribes and grew fruits and vegetables.

About A.D. 1200 the Quechua Indians began to conquer the weaker tribes in the area. They united them under one king, called the Inca.

In time, the name *Inca* was used to define the

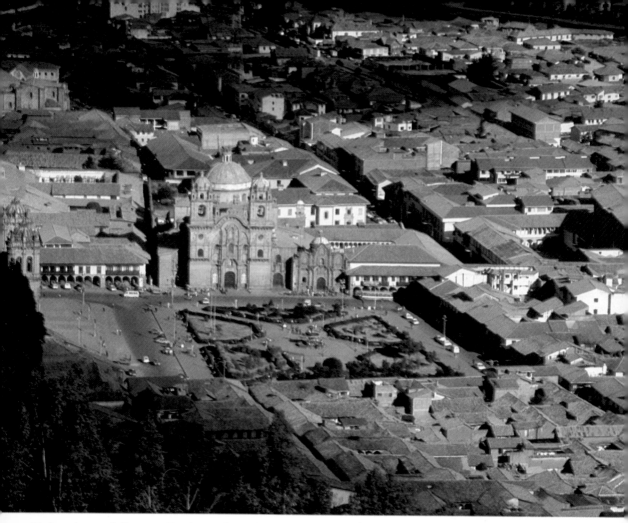
Main plaza at Cuzco. Pachacuti made Cuzco the center of the Inca Empire in 1438.

whole nation. It meant
"Children of the Sun."
Cuzco became the
capital city of the Inca.

In 1438 Pachacuti became the ninth Inca king. Pachacuti was a wise leader. Instead of killing young males from conquered tribes, he trained them to be Inca soldiers.

Because Pachacuti kept his men well fed, they remained loyal. The Inca civilization reached its peak under his leadership.

By the time Spaniards arrived in 1532, the Inca

Andes Mountains

Amazon River

Andes Mountains

THE INCA EMPIRE

The Inca Empire was one of the greatest civilizations in South America.

Empire covered over 2,500 miles and included twelve million people. It stretched from Ecuador to Chile. All the Inca people were united by one ruler, one language, and one way of life.

THE INCA PEOPLE

Spanish records say the Inca people were "lovely to behold." They had copper-colored skin, black eyes, and thick hair. The men stood about five feet, three inches tall, and the women a little under five feet tall.

Living in high altitudes helped the Inca develop strong lungs. They could work hard for long periods without becoming tired.

The people wore simple clothing woven of wool or cotton. Each peasant had two sets of clothing: one for every day and one for special occasions.

An Inca man wore a loincloth covered by a sleeveless overshirt that hung to his knees. A woolen cloak was used as a blanket on cool nights. The king wore the same clothing, but his was beautifully decorated.

The colorful woolen cloaks (left) and the panama hats (right)
are still worn by the descendants of the Inca.

An Inca woman wore an
ankle-length tunic tied with
a woven belt. She, too,
carried a cloak or shawl.
Both men and women
wore sandals or went

The Peruvian pottery vase (left) and the elaborate designs woven in cloth (right) are reminders of Inca culture.

barefoot. Women usually parted their hair in the middle and decorated it with combs and ribbons. Men wore their hair short with bangs.

INCA GOVERNMENT AND LAW

The king was the head of Inca government. He and his wife were believed to be part gods.

Although the king was all-powerful, he was advised by a High Council, made up of family members. Other members of the ruling class served the government. For every

10,000 people, there were 1,331 government officials. The king ruled as long as he lived. When he died, he was mummified and

Local chief at Pizac market and the remarkably well-preserved mummy (right) of a member of the Inca ruling class.

buried in his palace. His household servants were killed and buried near him. Sometimes the queen chose to die with her husband.

Most Inca families farmed shared land. These families were governed by an elected official who reported to a district leader. This person reported to a territorial leader, who answered to the king.

Each year the local leaders decided how much farmland each family needed. If a baby had been born, the family was given more land. If a family member had died or married, the amount of land was decreased.

Men aged twenty-one to forty-five had to work on government building projects and serve in the army. While a man was away serving the

Today the Inca use plows
pulled by work animals
to help them farm. But much
of the hard work is
still done by hand.

government, his neighbors
took care of his fields.

According to Inca law,
no person could go without
food, clothing, or shelter.
Every man, woman, and
child was expected to
work. Only the sick and
disabled were excused.

17

A portion of each harvest was given to the king for storage. If the crops failed, storehouses were opened and the people were fed.

Laziness was a crime against the king, equal to treason. Murderers and thieves were put to death. But if a thief could prove he really needed what he stole, the government official who had not taken care of him was punished.

GROWING UP AN INCA

Inca children were not named at birth. Instead, they were called *wawa,* which means "baby." At about age two, a child was given a nickname. At age thirteen or fourteen, a boy

began wearing a loincloth, a symbol of adulthood. At this time he chose a permanent name.

The sons of wealthy families were sent to Cuzco where they were educated to become members of the ruling class.

Near the age of fourteen, girls were given a hair-combing ceremony. Then they, too, chose permanent

Nineteenth century drawing of an Inca queen and princess (left). A modern-day Indian (right)

names. Afterwards they could marry. Beautiful or talented girls were often sent to Cuzco to become "Chosen Women." They were trained to be brides of the ruling class or to serve as temple priestesses.

Every man was expected to marry by the age of twenty. If he did not choose a wife, one was selected for him. An Inca wedding was simple. The bride and groom joined hands and exchanged sandals. A feast followed.

All the members of the community helped a young couple build their house. Inca houses were simple— one large room made of stones held together with mud. The grass roof had a

The Inca lived in small villages (above). All the houses had grass roofs and one doorway (left). The Indians still live in stone huts.

steep slope. There were no windows. The doorway was covered with a woolen cloth.

The Inca rose at dawn, ate food left over from the night before, then went to the fields. At mid-morning,

Corn (left) is still an important crop. Extra food crops are sold in the marketplaces.

they ate a meal of fruit, guinea pig, duck, corn on the cob, or potatoes.

Later, a snack of dried meat was eaten in the fields. At night the family ate a stew made from corn and chili peppers. Popcorn was as much a treat then as it is today.

The Inca cut terraces into the sides of mountains to prevent the good soil from washing away and to make irrigation easier.

FARMING AND HERDING

Inca farmers didn't use work animals. Yet, they were excellent farmers. They built terraces on the sides of mountains to

The descendants of the Inca grow the
same crops (above left), wear the same
style of clothes (above right), and herd alpaca
(below) in much the same way as their
ancestors did hundreds of years ago.

increase their farmland.
They dug canals for water
and used fertilizer.

In the desert lowlands
the main crops were
tomatoes, tropical fruit, and
cotton. In the mountains
the Inca grew potatoes.
After water was pressed
out of frozen potatoes, the
mush was dried in the sun.
It made a tasty meal.

High in the Andes
Mountains where crops
would not grow, the Inca
herded llama and alpaca.

Vicuña (left) and llama (right)

These animals supplied the Inca with wool and food.

Inca herdsmen cut the long wool from wild vicuña every year, then freed the animals. Only the king could wear clothing made from vicuña wool.

HIGHWAYS, MESSENGERS, AND BUILDINGS

The Inca built a 10,000-mile road system. They built roads through solid rock, over mountain gorges, and along desert plains. They did it all without the use of wheels or work animals.

The Inca built suspension bridges and pontoon bridges.

The suspension bridge (left) is attached to the stone foundations originally built by the Inca. This trail (right) leads to Machu Picchu.

Messages and packages were sent between cities by runners. All along the roads were huts about two miles apart. A runner waited in each hut. The messages and packages would be passed from one

In the ruins of an Inca noble's home visitors can see how running water was directed to the bath. The water at this bath has been running since the 1400s.

runner to the next. Inca runners were said to be able to cover 420 miles in three days.

Sacsahuaman, the great stone fortress at Cuzco, was built without the use of nails, wood, wheels, or work animals. Construction began in 1438. Thirty

The Sacsahuaman fortress like most large Inca buildings was made of polished stone that was cut out of the ground, placed on rollers, and pulled into place by thousands of workers.

thousand men worked on the job for seventy years.

The builders were so good that a knife cannot be slipped between any two stones—even after five hundred years!

RELIGION

The Inca were religious. Viracocha was their creator god. And Inti, the sun god, was the father of man. That is why Inca called themselves "Children of the Sun."

Everything in nature was related to a god or goddess—even gold and silver. Gold was the sweat of the sun. Silver was the tears of the moon.

The Incan god of air (above) and a
contest between the Incan gods of
earth and sea (right)

The ruling Inca's brother
or another relative served
as the high priest and
leader of all religious
ceremonies.

Priestly chores included
counseling, curing the sick,
and performing ceremonies.

The Inca believed signs
from the gods would tell
them what to do.

ARTS AND SCIENCES

Music was important.
During religious ceremonies
the priestesses danced
and sang.

Shepherds made wooden
flutes and played them to
calm their herds. Other

Inca instruments included bells, drums, tambourines, trumpets, hollow logs, and seashells.

The Inca were excellent artists. Craftspeople made jewelry, masks, and earplugs. Many of these

Inca women (below) made dyes from plants and wove cloth on looms. These gold objects (right), taken from an Inca grave, are examples of Inca art.

Modern-day craftspeople make and
sell Inca designs (left) and pottery (above).

products were sold in the
Inca marketplaces. Inca
pottery can be seen in
museums today.

The Inca believed that
all sickness was caused
by supernatural forces. Yet,
these same people

performed successful brain surgery. They also made medicines from herbs and roots.

To count, the Inca used a quipu. By making knots in the quipu's strings at different places, officials could count and keep records.

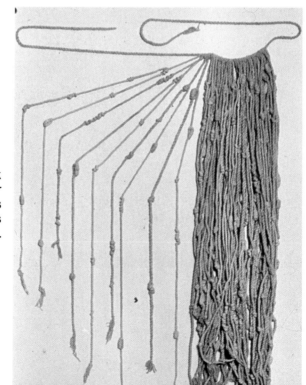

A quipu had one thick main string. Other strings of various colors and thickness hung from the main string.

THE END OF THE INCA EMPIRE

In May, 1532, Francisco Pizarro and 180 Spanish soldiers landed on the Pacific coast of South America. They had come looking for gold.

Atahualpa, the Inca king, agreed to meet with the Spaniards. When he entered Cajamarca, Peru, the Spaniards attacked by

Drawing of Inca soldiers taken from an ancient Peruvian vase

surprise. Hundreds of Inca were killed.

For the first time, the mighty Inca army met a force it could not defeat. Spears and shields were no match against Spanish cannons and metal armor.

Atahualpa (left) and Francisco Pizarro (right)

Also, the Spaniards rode horses, which the Inca had never seen before.

The Inca king was captured. Runners were sent throughout the kingdom with the message "Send gold to free

Atahualpa." Gold poured in from the four corners of the Inca Empire.

It is estimated that Pizarro received sixty-five million dollars worth of gold. Still, the Inca people could not save their king.

Atahualpa was held prisoner for months. Then in the summer of 1533, the Spaniards killed him.

The Inca revolted, but the Spaniards were too powerful. The revolt was

In 1596 Theodore de Bry drew this picture of Pizarro's soldiers attacking the Inca.

crushed. The measles, smallpox, and influenza— brought by the Spanish— killed thousands. By 1534 the mighty Inca Empire was completely under Spanish rule.

THE INCA TODAY

Today there are twenty
million Inca descendants
living in the highlands of
Peru. Some speak the ancient

Many descendants of the Inca live in cities and wear modern clothes.

language, wear the same
style of clothing, and have
much the same way of life
that their ancestors did
over five hundred years ago.

WORDS YOU SHOULD KNOW

altitude(AL • tuh • tood) — height; the distance of an object from the ground or from sea level

ancestor(AN • sess • ter) — a person from whom one is descended, usually back more than several generations

civilization(siv • uh • luh • ZAY • shun) — a high stage of culture developed over a period of time

community(kuh • MYOO • nut • ee) — a group of people living in the same area who have the same interests and life-style

descendants(di • SEN • dunts) — people who are related to the same ancestor

empire(EM • pie • er) — a large territory consisting of many people under the leadership of one government

fortress(FOR • trus) — a large place fortified against enemy attack

loincloth(LOIN • kloth) — a cloth worn around the loins, or the region of the hips, usually in a warm climate

loyal(LOI • ul) — faithful; true

mummified(MUM • ih • fyed) — embalmed; treated with preservatives before burial

nobility(no • BIL • uht • ee) — the people of the highest class in a country or civilization

overshirt(O • ver • shert) — a shirt worn over other garments, not tucked in at the waist

pottery(POT • uh • ree) — things made of clay, such as bowls, pots, dishes, etc.

priest(PREEST) — a man who performs religious rites

priestess(PREEST • ess) — a female priest, who performs religious rites

rain forest(RAIN FOR • est) — a tree-covered area in tropical lands with heavy annual rainfall; often called jungle

supernatural(soo • per • NACH • uh • rul) — relating to gods, spirits, ghosts, etc.

temple(TEM • pul) — a building used for religious services

terraces(TAIR • us • us) — steps up the side of a mountain on which crops are grown

tribe(TRYB) — a group of people of the same race, with the same customs, who band together under one leader

tunic(TOO • nik) — a simple, one-piece garment, with or without sleeves, usually very loose fitting

INDEX

About the author

Patricia C. McKissack and her husband, Fredrick, are freelance writers, editors, and teachers of writing. They are the owners and operators of All-Writing Services, located in Clayton, Missouri. Ms. McKissack, an award-winning editor, published author, and experienced educator, has taught writing at several St. Louis colleges and universities, including Lindenwood College, the University of Missouri at St. Louis, and Forest Park Community College.

Since 1975, Ms. McKissack has published numerous magazine articles and stories for juvenile and adult readers. She has also conducted educational and editorial workshops throughout the country for a number of organizations, businesses, and universities.

Patricia McKissack is the mother of three teenage sons. They all live in a large remodeled inner-city home in St. Louis. Aside from writing, which she considers a hobby as well as a career, Ms. McKissack likes to take care of her many plants.